JOAN OF ARKANSAS

JOAN
of ARKANSAS

EMMA WIPPERMANN

UGLY DUCKLING PRESSE
BROOKLYN, NEW YORK

Joan of Arkansas © Emma Wippermann, 2023

ISBN: 978-1-946604-02-6
First Edition, First Printing, 2023

Ugly Duckling Presse
The Old American Can Factory
232 Third Street, #E-303
Brooklyn, NY 11215
uglyducklingpresse.org

Cover art: Math Bass, *Newz!* 2019

Design: IngeInge
Printed and bound in East Peoria, IL by Versa Press

Distributed in the USA by SPD/Small Press Distribution
Distributed in the UK by Inpress Books

The publication of this book was made possible, in part, by
public funds from the New York City Department of Cultural
Affairs in partnership with the City Council, by the New York
State Council on the Arts with the support of the Office of
the Governor and the New York State Legislature, and by an
award from the National Endowment for the Arts.

for Pam and Laurel

seclusion and angels exist;
widows and elk exist; every
detail exists; memory, memory's light;
afterglow exists; oaks, elms,
junipers, sameness, loneliness exist;
eider ducks, spiders, and vinegar
exist, and the future, the future

—Inger Christensen

The beautiful, almost without any effort
of our own, acquaints us with the mental
event of conviction, and so pleasurable a
mental state is this that ever afterwards
one is willing to labor, struggle, wrestle
with the world to locate enduring sources
of conviction—to locate what is true.

—Elaine Scarry

Just hold me while I cry my eyes out
I'm not Joan of Arc, not yet

—Madonna

CONTENTS

———

THE LEGEND OF PETIT JEAN

Now if everyone could step onto the path   thanks
and the rare twistflower thanks you too

The Legend of Petit Jean   and I may say it
"petty jeen" but   you can imagine the French
would say it different   " pet-ee jz-ah "
                          " little   John "
John—Jean—so small   her first name
                          was Adrienne Dumont

So it's sometime in the 1700s

the twistflower thrives the camphorweed runs pink
in the moist   moonseed vines twist up the trunks
of trees—post oak   dogwood sweetgum

it's two hundred years
before Petit Jean State Park's founding

Arkansas isn't Arkansas yet   and this corner of it
is Osage land   or where they hunt
Quapaw to the east   and Caddo south

and Europeans are coming
and building and killing   with guns and disease

Poste aux Arkansas   *entrada*   *expédition*

fire as   whose deity

and a ship sails up the river

I don't know who called the river what then   there
isn't any info online   and the State Park
doesn't say   not surprising

anyway

a ship from France sails up the Arkansas River

            and Adrienne Dumont

            the fiancé
            of a member
            of the expedition

is in drag   aboard   working as a cabin boy

she is small
the crew call her
        Petit Jean
supposedly her fiancé didn't recognize her
in pants
he had intended
to leave her in France

There are three reasons Petit Jean
might have gotten on that ship:
        1. she loved her fiancé;
        2. she hated her fiancé;

3. she wanted to wear men's clothes
    and colonize the world

And sir   if you could step back onto the path
we'll walk now to the viewpoint
of Petit Jean Mountain where Petit Jean is buried
because see
she got off the boat   caught a disease
her fiancé found out   her identity
before she died   and she requested
to be buried   just here
you see   this mound
and marker   this mountain
and park   the tributary
that feeds   the Arkansas
are named   for the cabin boy
Petit Jean   Little John
a colonizer   and it wasn't
Jean's fault   the ships came
but Jean did   join them

and then   Jeanne died

And sir   if you could step back onto the path

the endangered   willow flycatcher
thanks you

            more information
            can be found
            at www.arkansasstateparks.com

JOAN OF ARKANSAS

CHARACTERS

JOAN
>   awkward teen
>   but adamantine
>   with grace
>   takes selfies
>   to self-abnegate
>   rly needs to feel
>   God's Hot Gaze

MOM OF JOAN
>   devoted
>   Arkansas State
>   Park Ranger

FATHER JOE
>   priest and bustling
>   busybody of Domremy

CHARLES VII
>   Governor (R) of Arkansas
>   and our potential president

CAMPAIGN MANAGER
>   oh everyone but
>   God needs one

REPORTER
>   a senstive sieve
>   of the news

ANGELS 1, 2, and 3
    Angels, also saints
    basically clouds

FOLLOWERS
    not a chorus
    but "the comment section"

PLACE

Domremy, Arkansas
in the increasing Heat
of the U.S.A.

TIME

The future, now—
or, Election Season
—but with the Medieval logic
of the Hundred Years' War

A NOTE ON STYLE

If performing, do it with a lot of speed; the spaces and line breaks are emphases; talk as fast as you can read. No one waits for anybody to finish speaking. Imagine a fifteenth-century brain on amphetamines with full knowledge that the earth is burning.

PROLOGUE

Alone in the dark
dark except for the white light of a phone
illuminating the face of JOAN in the foreground

The FOLLOWERS hum
a single note, a note that gets higher
with each new click, each like, a lick
with each new follow the note gets
higher and Hotter
and more—more FOLLOWERS join
as the hum becomes
Viral: a fever
then whine, a shriek suddenly
low, a single long
choral moan

                        until quiet

JOAN
O great
cloud of
witnesses!
Heaven or
internet it's
hard to be
good

            All the lights go off

I

The stage is set and a podium awaits

CHARLES VII enters
and walks to the podium
this is all for him—or, supposedly, for us

The CAMPAIGN MANAGER follows CHARLES VII
and stands some ten feet behind him

CHARLES VII
      Ladies and gentlemen
I hail   from the great state   of Arkansas!

There's a
smattering
of claps
from backstage

I have seen America at its best
and I have seen America put to the test *[winks]*
and I can say big government won't fix
what so sorely needs fixing!   Washington's after
your jobs!   your guns!   your God-given rights!
And I can say right now—taking away our freedom

won't fix these long years
of unnatural disasters   God knows!
Only jobs, guns, and natural liberties
Only our red-blooded   American families
can soothe the wounds
of this absolutely phantasmic loss
                    As Governor
                    I have lead Arkansas
                     in these turbulent times
                    And I will to lead America
                    in the worse times are that to come
                    —and yes! They're coming!
          So I am here today
          to announce my candidacy
          for President of the United States
I will be the Lord's candidate
          for President of this proud nation
I will be the Lord's candidate
          for President of the great USA
I will be the candidate of the Lord
          for the American people!
Thank you!
Yes, yes! Thank you, Jesus!
                    And may God bless America

Small applause comes from backstage

Exit CHARLES VII and CAMPAIGN MANAGER

Enter REPORTER
with microphone, cord dragging

REPORTER
Well, you heard it here first
Governor Charles VII of Arkansas
with no mention of the Warmth
has announced he's running on God's own
Republican ticket to save the nation
from unnatural disaster

[turns, points the microphone at the audience]

Do you think he—

[clears throat]

If the world is really—

[sweat forms on the brow]

Should someone save us?

[drops the mic]

Exit REPORTER

II

It's election season
and already scorching

In an unprecedented drought
the town of Domremy
is a dusty bin next to the Arkansas River
which recedes from its banks and flows without verve

Today is FATHER JOE's
Sunday morning mass

the FOLLOWERS and pious JOAN are in the pews

FATHER JOE is at the pulpit

and everyone sweats and sweats

FATHER JOE
Since we are
surrounded by such
a great cloud of witnesses—

    JOAN *[almost inaudibly]*
    —let us throw off all this sin
                 that entangles!

FATHER JOE
And let us run with endurance
the race set out for us—

JOAN
Amen!

FATHER JOE
And let us pray for those in our parish
for our sick and our needy and the nation
for our town   stricken by drought
Let us pray for Charles VII—the Lord's candidate
Arkansas's own Charles   who does
the Lord's good work   Thanks be to God

JOAN
And to you
          my good God

*Mass ends
and the FOLLOWERS and FATHER JOE exit*

*JOAN files out of the pew
and begins to walk very deliberately
alternately looking at their phone screen
and the low-slung
clouds above*

JOAN
Sweet God—

O glacial God I'm sorry!
Jesus
God and
        Angels
please   tell me
              again
              how I'm supposed to do it
              how I'm supposed to
convince the good Governor
              to get good policy
        to become the President
to save us all
              from the Warmth
O temperate God!
flanked by   Angels
        whose hair blows
              with Polar Easterlies
and Prevailing Westerlies
        Oh Angels!
who give the good saints
        their raptures
                          as they give me
                          mine

O good old growth God!
please help
keep me from sin
and complete your mission

Enter FATHER JOE
who begins walking beside JOAN
who jumps in surprise

FATHER JOE
May I drive you
home, Joan?

    JOAN
    Oh um
    thanks, Father Joe

FATHER JOE
So you
like the book of Hebrews?

    JOAN
    Yeah
    um

FATHER JOE
Good, good
Will I see you at the rummage sale on Wednesday?

JOAN
    Mh hm
    um—?

FATHER JOE
And what about your mother?
I rarely see her

    JOAN
      Yes
      well

FATHER JOE
Joan I see you're still wearing
your brother's
old clothes—Joan, you know
I'm sure there are some girls in your class—

    JOAN
        Father Joe?

FATHER JOE
Yes?

    JOAN
    What do you know
    about impossible-sounding
    heavenly instructions and exactly
    how to go about them?

FATHER JOE
Well, the Lord asks hard things of us

    JOAN
        So hard!

FATHER JOE
But it's never more than we—

    JOAN
        It might be impossible?

FATHER JOE
Nothing is impossible for the Lord!

JOAN
But for me?

FATHER JOE
Well the Lord does love you

JOAN
Yeah

FATHER JOE
Always remember that the Lord loves you!

JOAN
Yeah I know
They do

FATHER JOE
—they?

JOAN
Yeah, you know,
Them:
God
Angels
Mary, Saints, the good Holy Ghost
and
Jesus
Christ
our
Savior

FATHER JOE
Ah, the Trinity doesn't quite—

    JOAN
        Father Joe
        have you ever
        talked to Angels?

Before Father Joe can respond
they arrive at Joan's house,
small but sturdy
on a steep hill
basically overtaken by trees

Enter MOM OF JOAN
wearing her Park Ranger uniform:
buttoned khakis, a wide-brimmed hat
and golden badge

MOM OF JOAN
Joan!

    JOAN
    Hi Mom

MOM OF JOAN
Oh and it's you, Father Joe
so sweet of you to bring Joan
all the way home
I'm sorry I couldn't make it

to church
today—I patrol
on Sundays
you know
but Joan—can't
keep the kid away
—from church
I mean

FATHER JOE
Of course, well, Joan is
quite special in
well, what I call
a "Christ Connection"

MOM OF JOAN
I did always say
that if Joan was going
to go for god
pre-Luther was definitely
the best route

JOAN
Mom!!

MOM OF JOAN
Father, did you know that Joan
makes these videos on the internet?
Videos to God, apparently

JOAN
Mom!!!

FATHER JOE
Well um
any way to get the Lord's Word out…

MOM OF JOAN
I guess

FATHER JOE
Joan is a really special—

JOAN
Bye! Father Joe!

*MOM OF JOAN smiles brightly at JOAN
and JOAN exits
running up the yard and into the woods*

MOM OF JOAN *[turning quickly to FATHER JOE]*
Did you know that Joan
hears voices?

FATHER JOE
No…
No I did not

MOM OF JOAN
Yeah, well the voices
told Joan to stay a virgin so
they can't be too bad
but

FATHER JOE
They told Joan to—

MOM OF JOAN
Sorry, I mean
they told them to abstain
from penetrative sex
—something about a trial?
No sex and fight the Warmth so
all in all a good thing

FATHER JOE
Heavens, we really must pray
over this—please—come to church
I can teach you the prayers if you—

MOM OF JOAN
Ah yeah   I mean
of course   I pray
it's just work, you know
the state park is just
packed this time of year
everyone wants to be at Petit Jean
with the cool breeze at the top of that mountain—

FATHER JOE
Right right
you're over at Petit Jean State Park

MOM OF JOAN
First state park in Arkansas

FATHER JOE
Is that so
Well, some Sunday
or any weekday, really
drop by the church, Ms.—may I call you Isabelle?
Isabelle, it's good to receive
the sacraments

MOM OF JOAN
Sure
okay
so these voices that Joan hears—

FATHER JOE
Will Joan
have Confirmation
next year?

MOM OF JOAN
I don't think I could
keep them away
but—

From far away, from deep within the woods
they hear
in the voice of JOAN
a long

AHHHHHHHH!!

and a
SWEET GOD HOLY
ANGELS

SAINTS MARGARET AND CATHERINE
and again
AHHHHHHH!!!!
and then
a sob

MOM OF JOAN
Well!
I guess I should go

FATHER JOE
Of course

MOM OF JOAN
Thanks, Father
for bringing Joan home

FATHER JOE
Isabelle, it was a pleasure
        [touching her shoulder]
Call me Joe

FATHER JOE exits
and MOM OF JOAN walks up toward the house
then just past it
and stares into the expanse of woods

Everything is quiet now
but for the growing susurrus of forest

Everything is still now

but for JOAN, who walks in total rapture
slowly and wide-eyed
across the stage

MOM OF JOAN *[looking into the woods]*
Joan?

The stage gets darker
and quieter
everything is still and quiet and dark
until with a great crack
lightning lights everything up

MOM OF JOAN
Joan??

With a deep rumble
clouds move in

MOM OF JOAN   JOAN
Joan!!!!!!!!!   God!!!!!!!!!

III

In the forest, it's nighttime;
deciduous trees shake
large boulders take their places
among shadows and the mood
is serious, somber—but with a holy
fault line; the mood of a kid
in church
about to crack
up in
the company
of Angels

Enter REPORTER

REPORTER
Well, beauty does incite certainty!
And Joan—oh, Joan's certain
        They can't but equate the beautiful
        with event of conviction;
And these angels, they're beautiful
The Angels with their Voices are
        beautiful
Stay tuned, I hear
        they're training Joan
for the news ahead

Exit REPORTER

Enter ANGELS 1, 2, and 3
followed immediately by JOAN

ANGEL 1
So—
the Right Angel Congruence Theorem?

>JOAN
>All right Angels
>are congruent

ANGEL 2
Next:
Alternate Interior
Angels Theorem?

>JOAN
>If two parallel lives are
>cut by a transversal
>then...then the alternate interior
>Angels are congruent

>>ANGEL 3
>>And the parallel
>>lives are who?

>JOAN
>Me
>and Charles VII,
>—um?

ANGEL 1
No time!
And the alternate Angels
are interior to whom?

JOAN
Me…

ANGEL 2
And congruent to whom?

JOAN
The Warming Earth?

ANGEL 1
Tell me
what is the Inscribed Angel Property—

ANGEL 3
—also known as
the Central Angel Theorem?

JOAN
Well the measure of an Angel
inscribed in a circle
is half the measure
of the Arc it
intercepts

ANGEL 2
And who is the measure of the Arc?!

JOAN
Me!

ANGEL 3
And the interception?!

JOAN
Arkansas!

ANGEL 1
And the name of the inscription
of the measure of the Angel
who moves grace
through you?!?!

JOAN
Um

ANGEL 3
Come on,
the Inscribed Angel Property!

ANGEL 2
Joan, you have to learn this

ANGEL 1
It's Warm
and the time with Charles
is coming up quick

ANGEL 2
Joan, I've been meaning to tell you

that for the next step in all this
you'll need better lighting

      ANGEL 3
      And baby, maybe
      do something with your hair

Joan lifts a lock—

ANGEL 1
What have we been telling you, Joan
about all this business with the phone?

      JOAN *[aggrieved]*
      Optics, optics, optics

ANGEL 2
      "Therefore we have Joan
      who is photogenic
      and will die for
      our emission sins"

      ANGEL 3
      We need the people to understand
      Their always imminent closeness

ANGEL 1
In the spirit of apocalyptic times,
God is working with a logic of immediacy

ANGEL 2
The pixels of Their image must
illuminate the photons out in the world!

ANGEL 3
Carbon trapped the photons
and now their glittering Heat must
glance off You!

ANGEL 2
No no, Joan, just picture yourself
a painted icon

ANGEL 1
Use your words and your image!
Anchor this Warm present
though it flees with the speed
of a fingertip scrolling on a cool-feeling screen

ANGEL 2
And now...

JOAN
Don't go!

ANGEL 1
Sorry it's
God—Oh, no

ANGEL 3
Oh Joan, baby, it's
gonna get wet—

ANGEL 2
Be careful, dear—

the river—we're
sorry, Joan, it's God—

ANGEL 1, 2, and 3 *[together]*
They call!

Exit ANGELS with a quick sad glance at JOAN

*We hear the sounds of water: sloshing, trickling
then rain; rain starting in the way it does
when it won't stop for a long time*

And the ground's too dry to hold it

*JOAN looks at their phone
pauses in horror
and starts to run through the woods to home*

*Over brambles and branches
trees creaking from the sudden
wind at the canopy*

*The sky crackles and blackens
and JOAN is already soaked*

IV

*JOAN bursts through the door of the house
and the MOM OF JOAN cries out*

MOM OF JOAN
Joan!!!

    JOAN
    Mom!!!

MOM OF JOAN
    [rushing to embrace the wet JOAN]
Oh thank god you're safe

JOAN *[through the thick hug]*
Don't take the Lord's name in vain!

MOM OF JOAN
Well I meant it literally
even if it's his fault you were out there

    JOAN
    It's
    Their fault
    —Mom
    I saw the Angels again

MOM OF JOAN
Of course you did baby
well
what did they say?

    JOAN
    They gave me kind of a pep talk

MOM OF JOAN
A pep talk for what?

    JOAN
    I'm not sure you'll like it

MOM OF JOAN
You know I won't honey

    JOAN
    Ok well there's going to be
    flooding!
    By the river!
    We have to let people know and
    and—um—
            most importantly
      I need a haircut

MOM OF JOAN
Right now??

    JOAN
    [holding their phone out
        their arm a selfie stick

their eyes staring into the recording screen]

The sun's down on this side of the world
and still God loves us   though the sun
is down   and the water rises
over the flood stage   and into town
the storm pouring   from that great cloud
Witness:
      we can only bear this
by diluting   it in our minds;
    we have to stop diluting it
    so that we can't stand it

We know   the Warmth
We feel   the Heat
We see   the Problem
    come morning the sunlight
    the photons the trillions
glittering   off us trapped
down   here   with us
the carbon
O God
has said
elect Charles
to save
us all

     The lights dim

    Exit MOM OF JOAN

Enter FOLLOWERS walking in single-file;
each looking at the phone in their hands
they file across the back of the stage

JOAN sits on a stool in the middle of
the stage, positioned before
a semicircle of FOLLOWERS

there are puddles, watermarks, the dripping
joined by the sounds of scrolling, clicking

Enter MOM OF JOAN
she holds hair clippers; the cord drags

JOAN
Don't worry, Mom—
the Angels,
they'll love this

Enter ANGELS

ANGEL 1
And on this, the night of the flood
there cometh the viral video
and the subsequent followers
of Joan of Arkansas

ANGEL 2
The followers follow Joan

with dark hair shorn and
with a message to the nation
from God Themself

MOM OF JOAN *[tearily]*
But Joan's just
    a small speck serving
        the nation's need
           to sublimate

The rain beats down
on the house

MOM OF JOAN
turns on the clippers

and They hum

FOLLOWERS
ZzZZZzZzZzZzZzZzZzZzZzZzZzZzZzZz

MOM OF JOAN
MMMRRUUGGGGHHHHHHHHH

ANGEL 3
JOOOOOAAAN

FOLLOWERS
ZzZZZzZzZzZzZzZzZzZzZzZzZzZzZzZz

ANGEL 3
OF ARKANSAAASS!

Still holding out their phone
JOAN smiles
and MOM OF JOAN begins to shave

ANGEL 1
Oh   the note of the Mom of Joan's moan:
same as the buzzer

MOM OF JOAN
MMMRRUUGHHHHH

FOLLOWERS
ZzZZZzZzZzZzZzZzZzZzZzZzZzZzZzZz
ZzZZZzZzZzZzZzZzZzZzZzZzZzZzZzZz

All back slowly off the stage
leaving JOAN alone
with a new silhouette
sitting on the stool

JOAN
Hello?

JOAN looks out the dark window
where the rain soaks through the night

then looks at the blue-lit window
of their phone

FOLLOWERS *[from backstage]*
zzzzzzzzzzzzzzzzzzzzzzzzzzzzz

JOAN
Hello?
Uh   hello?
Oh   God
    witness
      viewer
         clouded
  flank of carnations
This   God's system floating
on the flood of Themselves
O   briefest
    expansion
    of heaven!
    I recognize You

V

It's been a day and a night

FATHER JOE and JOAN
are sitting in his office at school

Everything is wrecked from the flooding:
papers are wet and strewn
table legs have water marks

and FATHER JOE and JOAN sit upon
different desks
on either side of the stage

FATHER JOE
It's ok, Joan

      JOAN
      Ok

FATHER JOE
Joan
I've gotten some calls
from parents this morning

JOAN touches their head reflexively

FATHER JOE
No, it's not that
Joan
I mean, it's
          [he winks]
part of it, but um
Joan, I hear you've been
          [pauses, inhales]
that you, that your—
that your video has
gone viral?

     JOAN
     I'm viral

FATHER JOE
You've gone viral

     JOAN
     I am viral

FATHER JOE
Your video—

     JOAN
     Is viral
     like me
     via the Angels

FATHER JOE
The angels—?

JOAN
The Angels

FATHER JOE
In the video?

JOAN
I made the video

FATHER JOE
And the Angels?

JOAN
I talked to them
before the flood
before I made the video

FATHER JOE
...and your hair?

JOAN
They told me to do something with it

FATHER JOE
Angels told you to do that?

JOAN
They definitely
recommended it

FATHER JOE
It's not very

becoming
for um—a young
woman

JOAN
I'm not a young woman

FATHER JOE
Oh?

JOAN
I'm a messenger

FATHER JOE
Like in the video?

JOAN
The video was a message
via God via Angels
via me, the Messenger

FATHER JOE
So Joan
would you
explain your message

JOAN
God's message

FATHER JOE
Which is?

JOAN

Arkansas's own (R)
Governor Charles VII
will accept the past,
present, and ongoing
crisis of the planet and
act accordingly in regards
to the Warmth, escalating
devastation, genocidal
domestic and foreign
policies, and the Heat-
driven migration of those
whom this country has
systematically displaced
and through acceptance
of the Truth will be
by Our Lord's hands
compelled to action to
radicalize the Republican
party in favor of the
protection of God's earth
and Their people through
a platform of oil and coal
divestment, open borders,
sanctuary for all, and full
reparations of land and
goods; and by doing so,
Charles VII will win his
bid for president and
subsequently implement
said policies

FATHER JOE
Ok, Joan—

JOAN
Father Joe

FATHER JOE
Joan—I want to talk
about this message

JOAN
What about the message

FATHER JOE
Well, you know, the message…
and its presentation

JOAN
You mean God's message

FATHER JOE
OK— for the sake
of argument—"God's message"

JOAN
I'm the messenger

FATHER JOE
Uh huh

JOAN
And the message is from God

FATHER JOE
Sure

JOAN
So that's the message
and its presentation

FATHER JOE
Joan, you know
things like this they
have consequences

JOAN
Oh I hope they do!

FATHER JOE
I'm just worried for you
going after the Governor like this, I mean

JOAN
How can you be worried
when this is what God wants?

FATHER JOE
Well you may just be a bit
out of your league, Joan
politically and theologically

JOAN
Angels are not out of any league
[the school bell rings in the distance]
—speaking of which I have to go!

FATHER JOE
Go where?

JOAN
To the woods! They wait!

FATHER JOE
How can you be sure that—

JOAN
Bye Father Joe!

FATHER JOE
But—

JOAN
Sorry   They
hate when I'm late!

VI

JOAN is alone
on stage
in the woods

They're holding
a bucket of water

JOAN
           The Warmth is now
sucking the wet out of every flood-stain
in town   It's extra humid this year
like the flood never left   just
transcended
its form   like we'll
        breathe it all
        in all spring
     our town's drying up but
Mom's ranger uniform is sweaty after work
Our pores open and drip out
        the Arkansas River
My face in every drop of it
The Angels said something about
immolation   but I think
They must   have meant
Ascension   to heaven   my face
as a bunch of pixels

on everyone's phone
         Like the Arkansas River
came into the streets of Domremy
         I flooded
the internet
            The Angels said
            this world is
God's own
              narcissistic wound
but I think They were joking
about the trauma   of Creation
O I love God   and my mom
they both hold me
sometimes literally
and all the time figuratively
and I try to love every thumb that scrolls
I love everyone   who knows me
       as a photo   a mass of photons
I think I am the pleasure of God
The words type from my tongue
and God's lips open to a mouth
that's mine
Toes tucked and muscles taut to receive
God tells me and I say it
It's my job to say everything
           a mouth doesn't listen
God has an orifice   and it's powerful
Heaven   has the internet
every sigh heaved from every small sufferer
Mom watched me light   the
grill then light myself
a flash photo   for my followers

                              The soul is small
and knows nothing   but a damp sweat
a drop of gasoline   each prayer sends up
like a body   immolating
                    one radiant and unified Heat
a single flame   the smell of burning
                    hair and meat
The soul is in the smell
The sin is in   how bright

                                        the body burns

            Joan lifts
        the heavy bucket
            of water
        and slowly
            upends it
            over
        their head

VII

Enter CHARLES VII
followed closely
by the CAMPAIGN ADVISOR

CAMPAIGN ADVISOR
Um Sir I know how you feel about the internet but—

CHARLES VII
The internet but?

CAMPAIGN ADVISOR
Well your poll numbers just went up by fifteen percent

CHARLES VII
From the internet!

CAMPAIGN ADVISOR
There's a—kid?
On social media?
Joan—of Arkansas?

CHARLES VII
....?

CAMPAIGN ADVISOR
Joan talks to God?

CHARLES VII
And God says…

CAMPAIGN ADVISOR
Well God tells Joan
to tell people
to vote for you

CHARLES VII
Incredible!

CAMPAIGN ADVISOR
There was just a flood in Joan's town
I've scheduled a visit

Enter JOAN,
still soaking wet

JOAN
Well here you are in my small
and recently-flooded town

CHARLES VII
Joan, what a pleasure to meet you

JOAN
You call yourself the Lord's candidate

CHARLES VII
Straight to business, I see!

JOAN
This isn't business

CAMPAIGN MANAGER
Figure of speech, my dear

JOAN
If you are the Lord's candidate
you have to be against big business

CHARLES VII
Well, Joan, that's all very complicated

CAMPAIGN MANAGER
Leave the campaign issues to me, dear

JOAN
I can't

CHARLES VII
Oh?

JOAN
If you are the Lord's candidate
you have to do what the Lord wants

CHARLES VII
Of course I do
what the Lords asks of me

JOAN
Ok, well They ask that

you stop emissions
end drilling
welcome migrants
give land back and
provide reparations

CHARLES VII
Well, ah, Joan—

JOAN
Governor Charles VII

CHARLES VII
Well, Joan, the world is complicated
This is a complicated country and
you can't just
say things like that

JOAN
Not say, do

CHARLES VII
Ha! You can't just say things like that
and you especially can't do them
and expect to get elected

JOAN
I have 200 million followers

CHARLES VII
What?

JOAN
I have 200 million followers
not including the leagues
of Angels in heaven

CHARLES VII
Well, Joan, and I do thank you for your—

JOAN
Considering international
followers and those
who, like me, are too young to vote
approximately one third
of the expected voting populace
follows me

CHARLES VII
Well

JOAN
And by follows me I mean
I could lead them to you

CAMPAIGN MANAGER
Now that's more—

JOAN
God, the Angels, my Followers and I
expect you to do this

CHARLES VII
Ah—

JOAN
If you do this
you will be president

CHARLES VII
I don't know about that

JOAN
You will be a president
who does these things

CHARLES VII
But

JOAN
You will be the Lord's President

CHARLES VII
I can't just do any of that!

JOAN
Aren't you the candidate of the Lord?

CHARLES VII
How do I know you're right?

JOAN
How do you know God's right?

CHARLES VII
You're not God

JOAN
Obviously!
I'm Their messenger

CHARLES VII
Or maybe you're a crazy
liberal cross-dressing sinner
with devils in your ear!

JOAN
Ugh
I would never speak with the Devil
the Angels warned about this—I guess
I'll just have prove it to you

CHARLES VII
Now how might you do that

JOAN
Send me to campaign for you

CHARLES VII
What

JOAN
Send me to North Carolina
to campaign for you

CHARLES VII
That's impossible!
you might be a heretic

JOAN
OK
send me to a priest
have him question me
then send me to North Carolina
then California
it's going to be a swing state

CAMPAIGN MANAGER
What! That's absurd

JOAN
In two days check the news

CAMPAIGN MANAGER
How could you know that

JOAN
Are you listening to me??
I talk to Angels

CHARLES VII
Well

JOAN
This is a good idea

CAMPAIGN MANAGER
This might be a good idea

CHARLES VII
But how would it look

if I have this bald and
blasphemous child—

>CAMPAIGN MANAGER
>It might look
>like winning

JOAN
I would never blaspheme

>CAMPAIGN MANAGER
>I'm calling a priest

JOAN
I'll win you the election

>CAMPAIGN MANAGER
>You know, Joan
>Charles is quite…
>behind in the polls

>*CHARLES VII scoffs and bristles*

>JOAN [*to the CAMPAIGN MANAGER*]
>I know
>you really need me

CHARLES VII
I need no such thing!

CAMPAIGN MANAGER
This may be actually
precisely the thing

JOAN
You say you are
the Lord's candidate
but you aren't
listening to the Lord
people can sense that

CAMPAIGN MANAGER
Yes
and—

CHARLES VII
No!!!

JOAN
Yes

CHARLES VII
You—

JOAN
God

CHARLES VII
This platform—

JOAN
God's platform

CHARLES VII
I—

    JOAN
    You, the Lord's candidate

CHARLES VII
I…. support reparations?

    JOAN
    The Lord supports reparations
    and returning the land
    and open borders
    and prison abolition
    and ending fossil fuels and

CHARLES VII
Enough!!!

    JOAN
    It's not enough
    but it's a start

CHARLES VII
First the priest

    JOAN
    Great!

CHARLES VII
First the priest
then we'll see what he says

JOAN
I love priests!
and priests love me

VIII

Enter the FOLLOWERS
who carry a table and three chairs
to the center of the stage
then scatter about

Enter CHARLES VII and the CAMPAIGN
MANAGER
who sit down behind the table

Enter JOAN
who walks and stands before the table

Everyone is quiet
until FATHER JOE enters

CHARLES VII [*waving*
      from his chair and gesturing
      toward the empty seat beside him]
Father! Wonderful to
meet you, thank you
for coming on such
short notice

      FATHER JOE [*sitting down*]
      Joan?

JOAN
Hi Father Joe

CAMPAIGN MANAGER
You know Joan?

FATHER JOE
Well, I'm the town's priest

CHARLES VII *[clearing his throat]*
If Joan and the Father know each other
is this still a proper divinity test?

CAMPAIGN MANAGER
Father, um, are you
biased towards Joan?

FATHER JOE
I am an impartial servant of the Lord
—and you are?

CAMPAIGN MANAGER
I'm a partially serviced campaign servant

CHARLES VII
Well now we just want to know—

FATHER JOE
If her visions tell the truth?

CHARLES VII
Well yes

CAMPAIGN MANAGER
We can't send a tomboy
devil-whisperer out to
serve the will of other
campaigns
now, can we?

JOAN
I loathe the Devil

FATHER JOE
Do you talk
to the devil, Joan?

JOAN
The Devil talks to all of us
then takes our money

FATHER JOE
Joan, you really can't expect me to—

CAMPAIGN MANAGER
A simpler question, Father:
Crazy? Yes or no

FATHER JOE
Now, I'm no psychologist
and Joan is one
of the most
...enthusiastic
members of my parish

CAMPAIGN MANAGER
Well as we say in politics
fanaticism doesn't preclude craziness

FATHER JOE
I don't think Joan is…crazy

JOAN
Why would God choose
a crazy person
to be Their messenger?

CAMPAIGN MANAGER
Why do you keep talking about God in the plural???

CHARLES VII
That certainly sounds
polytheistic to me

JOAN
There is only one God
and we are all Their children

FATHER JOE
Ok, Governor, Joan—
Joan, are you a virgin?

CHARLES VII and the CAMPAIGN MANAGER
turn to look inquisitively first
at FATHER JOE then at JOAN

JOAN
Of course
the Angels said I must be

FATHER JOE
Must be a virgin?

JOAN
Must be unpunctured
and in potentia: nothing goes in
and God's messages come out

CHARLES VII
Ok, this is just too much
        [to the CAMPAIGN MANAGER]
let's wrap this up

JOAN
But

CAMPAIGN MANAGER *[looking at his phone]*
I would but
there's no cell service!

CHARLES VII
Jesus Christ just use wifi!

JOAN
Language!

CAMPAIGN MANAGER
There's no wifi either!

FATHER JOE
Aren't we in the middle of a divinity test?

CAMPAIGN MANAGER
I have a campaign to run!!

CHARLES VII [to the CAMPAIGN MANAGER]
Just get me the hell out of here

JOAN glares reproachfully

CAMPAIGN MANAGER [to FATHER JOE]
Do you have any service?

FATHER JOE looks at his phone and shakes his head

CAMPAIGN MANAGER [to a FOLLOWER]
Excuse me, is your phone working?

Looking at their phone
the FOLLOWER shakes their head no

JOAN
I forgive you your linguistic sins, Charles
So when will you announce
that I'm joining you on the campaign trail?

CAMPAIGN MANAGER
Likely never, sweetheart
and especially not if
the internet doesn't work

JOAN
I can make it work

CHARLES VII
Well why didn't you say something, kid!

JOAN
Type a post about me

CHARLES VII
What?

JOAN
Tell people about me

The CAMPAIGN MANAGER
rolls his eyes
and walks around
holding his phone into the air like a divining rod

CHARLES VII
I could, but it simply wouldn't send

JOAN
Type it, and I'll make the internet come back

CHARLES VII
That's absurd

CAMPAIGN MANAGER
Oh just do it
it'll make the kid shut up

CHARLES VII *[rolling his eyes
and typing on his phone]*
I am happy to announce
that Joan—

JOAN
—of Arkansas

CHARLES VII *[sighs]*
—will be joining my
upcoming
campaign events

JOAN
Please tag me

CHARLES VII
Fine—"at" Joan of Arkansas…

JOAN
Ok it sent

*The FOLLOWERS all simultaneously
check their phones*

CAMPAIGN MANAGER
What?

The FOLLOWERS look up
and around
and furiously begin typing

CHARLES VII
By God it did

JOAN
That's exactly how!

CAMPAIGN MANAGER
This means

CHARLES VII
We can delete it!

JOAN
The rest of the internet
should work now too

The FOLLOWERS are typing and pacing
and scrolling through their screens
the stage is inundated with clicks and ticks and pings
and palpable Heat

CAMPAIGN MANAGER
Ah it already has more likes
than all our other posts
possibly all our other posts combined

CHARLES VII
We can't delete it?

CAMPAIGN MANAGER *[strained]*
We can't delete it

> JOAN
> Congratulations!
> You're now the Lord's Candidate!
> Where are we going first?

IX

MOM OF JOAN and JOAN
are in a department store
shopping for a campaign outfit for JOAN

It's not going well

MOM OF JOAN *[picking up a sweater set]*
What about this?

    JOAN
    No!

MOM OF JOAN
Ok, I mean I know it's a little
"catalogue company" but
you need some nice things for the campaign

    JOAN
    I don't need nice clothes to fight the Warmth

MOM OF JOAN
I'm just following the instructions
of the invisible angels you insist speaking for

MOM of JOAN holds up a blouse

JOAN *[fake retches]*
Too churchy

MOM OF JOAN
I mean—

JOAN
Like "church girl"
I'm not a church girl
I'm a messenger
I'm—

MOM OF JOAN
You know, I think I'm getting it

JOAN
Clothes are terrible

MOM OF JOAN
Clothes aren't the point
they're the process

JOAN
Let's just go

MOM OF JOAN
I mean take my Park Ranger uniform
[she gestures at her wide-brimmed hat]

JOAN
Yeah um
Embarrassing

MOM OF JOAN
You can't wear your brothers' old clothes forever, Joan

JOAN
They'll always have old clothes

MOM OF JOAN
It represents a non-choice

JOAN
I'm choosing them!

MOM OF JOAN
No you are submitting
to the choices of your brothers
who first chose to wear the clothes
and then chose to get rid of them

JOAN
The Angels say—

MOM OF JOAN
I know I know
consumerism is bad etc.

JOAN
Actually it's mostly
the internet that says that
The Angels say—I don't really get it but—
they say that "my image will be
both the apex and end of me"

MOM OF JOAN
Wow   ok
but   honey
they also said you need new clothes
        [sees something in the distance]
I have an idea

        JOAN
        No more ideas they all lead to the destruction
        of God's planet!

MOM OF JOAN *[walking over to the boy's section
                    and holding up a suit]*

Try this on

        JOAN
        What

MOM OF JOAN
It's a suit

        JOAN
        Mom

MOM OF JOAN
Just try it on
        it's not going to fit right
                but we'll get it tailored

        JOAN
        Mom

MOM OF JOAN
Ok, ok, I just thought—

JOAN
Mom
I really love it

MOM OF JOAN
That's great, baby!

JOAN *[walking over to a suits]*
And Mom this vest thing?

MOM OF JOAN
The waistcoat?

JOAN
Can it be shiny

MOM OF JOAN pulls out a credit card and exits

The stage goes dark
then brightens just
to the glow of twilight

Wearing the new suit
JOAN runs out of their house
towards the forest

And in the half-light of the woods
the waistcoat gleams

Enter ANGELS 1, 2, and 3

ANGEL 1
Now that's more like it

> ANGEL 3 *[holding ANGEL 2's arm]*
> Oh! Our baby!

ANGEL 2
Joan, you look
absolutely
divine

ANGEL 1
Ok Joan
now—the phone

> *JOAN pulls out their phone*
> *their arm a selfie-stick*
> *and starts to move through the trees*

ANGEL 2
We want POSES!

> ANGEL 3
> The LORD GOD
> wants poses!

ANGEL 1
Say it to the world now, Joan

JOAN
[walking until their feet
meet the edge of the stage]
Hi

They turn
and take a selfie
with us
in the background

X

JOAN enters
wearing business casual
and is closely followed by
the FOLLOWERS, the REPORTER,
CHARLES VII, the CAMPAIGN MANAGER,
FATHER JOE, and ANGELS 1, 2, and 3

MOM OF JOAN enters last
carrying an impossibly tall pile of packages

REPORTER
What happens now
is both breaking news and ancient history

CAMPAIGN MANAGER
Do we have to go through this whole thing?

REPORTER
What happens now
is the realization that today was
all along
the good old days

FATHER JOE
We agreed to go through the whole story!

JOAN
Mom, why are you holding all those packages?

MOM OF JOAN
It's for later, baby, don't worry about it

CHARLES VII
I have a country to run, you know

CAMPAIGN MANAGER
The greatest country on earth

CHARLES VII
You don't work for me anymore!!

REPORTER [*points the microphone at CHARLES VII*]
A shocking event
in the strangest campaign
we've seen in decades!

CAMPAIGN MANAGER
Hey Father, ask the question

FATHER JOE
I thought we were going to run through the whole
story

CAMPAIGN MANAGER
Oh I'll ask—Joan, where are your angel friends now?

JOAN gestures toward ANGELS 1, 2, and 3

The ANGELS busily cast their gazes about
but everyone just looks
at the negative space
between them

CAMPAIGN MANAGER *[scoffs]*
So why didn't your invisible friends help you out?
Seems they hushed up right when you needed them

JOAN
God's quiet when They trust you the most

CAMPAIGN MANAGER
So God's been trusting me my whole life!

CHARLES VII
Can someone get rid of him?

A FOLLOWER takes the CAMPAIGN MANAGER
by the arm
and escorts him offstage

CHARLES VII
That guy gave just the worst advice
[turning to the REPORTER] If we're going to do this
let's get it over with

FATHER JOE
Great, let's start with my sermon

MOM OF JOAN
Joe, let's start with these packages

FATHER JOE
I'd rather you call me Father

MOM OF JOAN *[dropping the pile*
of packages to the floor]
So is "Joe" only for days you're evangelizing?

JOAN *[laughing]*
Oh Father, you never had a chance

FATHER JOE *[to JOAN]*
It's no wonder you turned out like you did!

MOM OF JOAN
Like a teenager who dies trying to fight the Warmth?

CHARLES VII
Now now
we haven't established the facts here

JOAN
Mom!!
Will you tell me what's in the packages?

MOM OF JOAN
I can't believe you ever helped that Heat-denier

JOAN
But God—

MOM OF JOAN
God's got nothing on life baby

FATHER JOE
God our Father is the creator of life

JOAN
The Angels said Creation
gave God PTSD

FATHER JOE *[sputtering]*
Wha—

CHARLES VII
As the Lord did—

REPORTER *[holding the microphone]*
President Charles VII, after taking Joan of
Arkansas into your campaign, winning the
election by a landslide largely thanks to Joan's
help, and then reneging on every promise you
made in relation to the Warmth, the borders,
reparations, and returning the land, do you still
believe you qualify as "the Lord's Candidate"?

CHARLES VII
Well now, I'd have say I'm no longer
the Lord's Candidate
but the Lord's President

FATHER JOE
You better be careful with that possessive "s" now

JOAN
Mom...?

MOM OF JOAN
Yes baby these packages are for you

The FOLLOWERS perk up

JOAN
Who are they from?

MOM OF JOAN
Your supporters, I guess

The FOLLOWERS surround them, beaming

FATHER JOE *[lifting a package to read it's address]*
To Joan of Domremy, Arkansas ... To the Virgin Saint
To Saint Joan ... our Savior... Joan! This is—

JOAN *[horrified]*
Is that heresy?

MOM OF JOAN *[opening a package]*
Looks like a Prada jacket to me

FATHER JOE
This is heresy!!!

MOM OF JOAN *[opening another package]*
Or it's an Hermès pocket square

JOAN
Father, I didn't ask for this!

FATHER JOE
Your pride, Joan, your pride asked for this

JOAN
Is it pride to do what God asks?

> ANGEL 1 *[whispering to JOAN]*
> No honey, but put on the Prada jacket

> *ANGEL 2 slips the jacket onto JOAN's shoulders*
> *while ANGEL 3 slips the pocket square in place*

MOM OF JOAN *[oblivious to the ANGELS]*
Joan, it's called strength of character

CHARLES VII
Now that all these
obviously pressing matters
are cleared up
I have a country to run

JOAN *[pleading]*
Please Charles

CHARLES VII
Now Joan
What's done is done

REPORTER *[into the microphone]*
In a shocking turn of events—

JOAN *[dropping to their knees]*
Charles, please!! You're the only one—
Someone has to do something
Someone has to fight it
Someone needs to stop the Warmth and

Two FOLLOWERS
walk up to JOAN
and take off JOAN's jacket
unbutton their shirt
unhook their belt
drop their pants
and place a hospital gown
upon JOAN's body

REPORTER
We'll look now at the initial scene of betrayal

CHARLES VII walks to the center of the stage
everyone else arranges themselves
as an audience and claps

CHARLES VII
Thank you, thank you
This is an historic moment
for our great country
as we embark
with my inauguration
on a journey with God
Tomorrow we will begin to keep
the promises to make America greater
stronger and running on American fuel

JOAN *[from the audience]*
Charles, no!!

CHARLES VII *[clearing his throat]*
Yes, we will be tough on those
who are soft on the American economy
which means strengthening our borders
and holding on to what's ours

JOAN
Charles, how could you??

CHARLES VII *[chuckling softly]*
It isn't easy to be righteous, but
we will strengthen the American family
by fighting those who seek to disrupt it
This is God's America now
and I am His President

JOAN rushes toward CHARLES VII

and the CAMPAIGN MANAGER enters
at a run from backstage
and tackles JOAN to the ground

CAMPAIGN MANAGER *[still on top of JOAN]*
I got her, Sir

MOM OF JOAN
Joan!!

The FOLLOWERS gasp collectively
aiming their phones
toward JOAN
who is still pinned down

CHARLES VII
Mental illness isn't the fault of the ill

MOM OF JOAN
They aren't crazy and you know it you—

CAMPAIGN MANAGER
Guards!

JOAN
[at a whisper] God!

JOAN's head falls to the floor

ANGELS 1, 2, and 3 slowly approach
JOAN's body is limp and the Angels lift them

The hospital gown flaps and flutters and flows

Singing, the ANGELS carry JOAN to the proscenium

ANGEL 3
Holy holy holy

ANGEL 2
All the saints adore thee

ANGEL 1
Casting down their golden crowns
around the glassy sea

FATHER JOE *[joining in]*
Holy holy holy

MOM OF JOAN *[through tears]*
Though the darkness hide thee

[all together]
Though the eye of sinful man
thy glory may not see—

All the lights go off

THE TRIAL
OF JEANNE D'ARC:

SOME EXCERPTS

THE TRIAL OF JEANNE D'ARC

TRANSLATED INTO ENGLISH

FROM THE ORIGINAL LATIN AND
FRENCH DOCUMENTS

BY W. P. BARRETT

GOTHAM HOUSE, INC.

1932

HERE BEGIN THE PROCEEDINGS AGAINST A DEAD WOMAN JEANNE

It has pleased divine Providence
that   the woman known as Jeanne

should be taken   apprehended
by famous warriors

The reputation of this woman
has already gone forth

and having thrown off
the bonds   of shame

she wore
with an astonishing   and monstrous
                      brazenness
immodest garments
belonging to the male sex;   moreover

she was not afraid to perform speak and
disseminate
many things   she is

guilty   of no inconsiderable offense

THE OFFICERS APPOINTED
TAKE OATH

Now when   men   as numerous as famous
were gathered   together   we
dispatched   the woman
burning with desire   we
surrendered   this woman
her idolatries
and unnumbered inconveniences
     such an enormous hurt
has not occurred   within human memory

     Heresy is a disease
which creeps
like cancer
secretly killing   the simple
unless the knife
of the inquisitor
cuts it away

THE FIRST PUBLIC SESSION

Wednesday, February 21 1431
at eight o'clock in the morning

vehement suspect
of heresy
she humbly begged   you

reverend father

to permit her to hear Mass

Decision : in view of the crimes

       of which this woman was defamed

       especially the impropriety
       of the garments to which she clung

it was their opinion that we should properly defer
permission
for her
to hear Mass

in her own country she was called Jeannette

and after   she was called Jeanne
Of her surname she knew nothing
she was born in the village of Domrémy

THURSDAY, FEBRUARY 22.

SECOND SESSION

we entered the Robing Room
where there were assembled the reverend fathers lords
and masters

The said Jeanne was then brought before us
and we admonished her   to take the oath

She answered: "you overburden me"

She replied: "If you were well informed about me
                  you would wish me to be
                  out of your hands"

Afterwards she declared that at the age of thirteen
she had a voice from God   And the first time
she was much afraid   And this voice came
                                  towards noon
                                  in summer in her garden

She said
that if she was in a wood she easily heard the voices

and she believed it was sent from God

FEBRUARY 24.

THIRD SESSION

and we thrice admonished her
And she added: "you overburden me"

and she would willingly speak the truth
but not the whole truth

Again we required her to swear
        precisely and absolutely

she answered: "I am more afraid of failing the voices
        than of answering you"

she answered that she had a great desire

for her king to have his kingdom

        Asked if she had wanted to be a man
        she said she had answered elsewhere

FEBRUARY 27.

FOURTH SESSION

Asked if the voices
Asked if the angels

spoke at the same time

she answered: "I have not leave to tell you"

Asked if she saw
these angels corporeally
                              and in reality

she answered: "I saw them with my bodily eyes
                              as well I see you;
                              and when they left
                              I wept"

Asked if God
ordered her to wear a man's dress

she answered that the dress is a small   nay
                              the least thing

she did not put it on but
                              by the command of angels

MARCH 1.
FIFTH SESSION

Asked if she herself did not have some rings

she replied: "You have one of mine; give it back to me"

MARCH 3.

SIXTH SESSION

Asked if   the queen did not inquire
                            about her taking
                            to a man's dress
she answered: "I do not remember"

Asked if   her king or queen did not
                            sometimes ask her to put off
                            her man's dress
she answered: "That is not in your case"

Asked if   others did not offer her
                            woman's dress
she answered   that others had often
                            asked her to wear it

Asked whether   God revealed to her
                            that she should change
                            to a man's dress
she answered: "You will learn no more
                            for the present"

Asked of   what material

she answered: "white satin, and on some
                            there were fleurs-de-lys"

Asked whether   the good wives did not touch
                       her ring with their own
she answered: "many women touched
                       my hands and rings; but I do
                       not know with what intention"

Asked whether   she received the sacraments
                       in man's dress

she answered yes   but does not remember
                       receiving them
                       when she was in armor

MARCH 10.
FIRST SESSION IN PRISON

Asked who had given her this horse

she answered her king

MONDAY MARCH 12 .

IN PRISON

The Vicar of the Lord Inquisitor is summoned

we the aforesaid bishop repaired
to the chamber   assigned as jail
for the said Jeanne

Asked whether the angel that brought the sign
Asked whether the angel did not fail her
Asked whether the angel did not fail her in respect
     of the good things of grace

     she answered: "How should he fail me
     when he comforts me everyday?

Asked whether she spoke to   Our Lord
when she promised   to keep her virginity

She added that the first time she heard her voice
     she vowed to keep her virginity
     ; and she was then thirteen years old

THE AFTERNOON OF THE SAME

MONDAY, IN PRISON

The said Jeanne   concerning the dreams
she declared her father had had   that Jeanne
his daughter   would go off with men-at-arms

Asked whether it was at the request
of Robert de Baudricourt
            that she first took to a man's dress

she answered that it was of her own accord
           and not at the request of any man alive

Asked whether the voice ordered her
          to wear a man's costume

she answered: "Everything I have done I have done
      at the instruction of my voices;
      as to the dress
      I will answer another time"

Asked whether she thought she was doing wrong
in taking
to male attire
      she answered no;

WEDNESDAY MARCH 14 .

IN PRISON

She answered   "You say that you are my judge;
I do not know if you are;

And beyond this   the voices told her

that she will be delivered
by a great victory; and then they said:

"Take everything

peacefully;   have no care for thy martyrdom"

And this her voices told her simply and absolutely
that is   without faltering

and she knows not whether she shall
yet suffer   greater adversity

but therein   she commits herself to God

THAT SAME WEDNESDAY
MARCH 14 . IN PRISON

And the said Jeanne first answered
that   she kept her oath and promise
to the   Our Lord   that is
to keep safe her virginity of body and of soul

And when she was reminded
                that she wore a man's dress
she was asked whether she did not believe she had
                committed mortal sin

"I do not think I am in mortal sin"

And secondly, concerning the horse

And fourthly, concerning the man's dress she wears

"I do it by God's command"

THURSDAY MARCH 15.

IN PRISON

in the prison   of the said Jeanne
The said Jeanne was charitably admonished
and required to be willing

Asked since she had wished to hear Mass
whether it did not seem   more fitting
      to be in female costume

Asked if in battle she had done anything without

     the permission of her voices

Asked how she recognized that they were angels

Asked how she would tell   a good or bad spirit

Asked about the height and stature of this angel

    she said she will reply on Saturday

SATURDAY MARCH 17.

IN PRISON

Asked on the subject of the woman's dress offered her
so that she might hear Mass

she answered that she would not put it on
till it should please Our Lord

Asked what warrant and what help she expected
to have from Our Lord
        by the fact that she wore man's dress

she answered that in this as in other things she sought
        only the salvation of her soul

                with the sword she won
out of devotion

THE AFTERNOON OF THE SAME DAY, IN PRISON

Asked what part of St. Catherine she had touched

she answered: "You will get no answer from me"

Asked if she ever kissed or touched

St. Catherine or St. Margaret

she answered she had touched them both

Asked if they had a fine odor   she answered

it is well known that they had

Asked whether   when embracing them

she felt heat or anything else

she answered that she could not embrace them

without feeling and touching them

PALM SUNDAY MARCH
THE TWENTY-FIFTH

Jeanne asks permission to receive
the sacrament of the Eucharist on Easter Sunday

as for changing her dress she could not
and it was not in her

adding that this attire
did not burden her soul

HERE BEGINS THE ORDINARY TRIAL

to the end that she should be declared a witch
enchantress false
prophet   a caller-up of evil spirits
superstitious implicated in and given to magic arts
thinking evil in our Catholic faith schismatic in the
article Unam Sanctam etc. and in many other articles
of our faith skeptic devious sacrilegious scandalous
seditious   perturbing and obstructing the peace
inciting to war cruelly thirsting for human blood
encouraging it to be shed   having utterly and
shamelessly abandoned the modesty befitting her sex
and indecently put on the ill-fitting dress and state
of men-at-arms;   and for that and other things
abominable to God and man

she should be punished

THE ORDINARY TRIAL

Here follows   word for word the tenor
       of the articles of accusation

I   she will   submit only
       to the Church in Heaven

II   certain people
       have kissed her hands and garments

III   infected with heresy
          and actually heretical

IV   as for the fairies
          she did not understand

VI   Jeanne was wont
       to frequent   the tree
          mostly at night

XII   with her hair cropped short and round
       like a young fop's,
       she wore shirt,
       breeches,
       doublet,
       with hose joined and fastened

by 20 points,
long leggings
laced on the outside,
a short mantle reaching to the knees,
or thereabouts,
a close-cut cap,
tightfitting boots,
and buskins,
long spurs,
sword,
dagger,
breastplate,
lance
and other arms in the style of a man-at-arms,
with which she performed actions of war
and affirmed
that she was fulfilling the commands of God

XIII   wearing short, tight, and dissolute male habits

        those underneath the breeches
as well as the rest;

and   she often dressed in
rich and sumptuous habits
precious stuffs
and cloths of gold and furs;
        and not only did she wear
short tunics
but she dressed herself in tabards
        and garments
open at the sides

whilst it is notorious
that when she was captured
she was wearing a loose cloak of cloth of gold
a cap on her head
and her hair cropped round in man's style

XIV "The said Jeanne affirms that it was right so to
wear garments and habits of dissolute men;
and will persist therein"

XV the aforesaid voices and spirits
consecrated her virginity

And she has touched them bodily
and felt them

XVI As for the other womanly duties

she says there are
enough other women to do them

XVII Jeanne replied she bore to her king
news from God
would have him crowned
would expel his enemies

She was God's messenger
to that effect;

XXII

I am "chef de guerre"

LIV   as for where she lodged
         she usually had a woman with her;
               when she was fighting
         she would lie fully dressed and armed
         if there was no woman
              to be found

LX   beautiful revelations

    I have sworn not to utter

WEDNESDAY MAY 23

the clergy declare

that you blaspheme against God

that you are full of vain boasting

that you are given to idolatry

and worship yourself and your clothes

we beg exhort and advise you

by the bowels of Our Lord Jesus Christ

THURSDAY MAY 24.

JEANNE RECANTS

the said Jeanne was present before us on a scaffold
        or platform

in the presence of a great multitude of people
she pronounced her recantation according
to the formula

: "I confess
that I have sinned in   pretending to have had
revelations
from God His angels ; in seducing others;
in wearing ill-shaped and immodest dress
and hair cropped
round like a man's   ; also in bearing arms
most presumptuously "

Signed: "Jehanne +"

She was given woman's dress
and allowed her hair which had hitherto
been cut short round the ears
to be shaved and removed

THE TRIAL FOR RELAPSE

Monday, May 28
Jeanne resumes man's dress

On Monday following the said judges repaired
to Jeanne's prison   to observe her

     the said Jeanne was wearing a man's dress a
short mantle
a hood a doublet and other garments   used by men

     we questioned her
Jeanne said she rejected woman's clothes

Asked why   she answered
     she preferred man's to woman's dress

She was told that she had promised not to wear
man's dress again
and answered   she never meant to take such an oath

She said   in truth she was sent from God

She said   what she had declared and recanted on
Thursday

    was done only for fear of the fire

TUESDAY MAY 29

Jeanne had   once more

        rejected woman's dress

the lords and masters
      the judges

declared Jeanne relapsed

declared   should be condemned
      as a heretic

declared   a relapsed heretic

no prayer for mercy

no prayer for mercy

she had always been a heretic

     and was in fact relapsed

relapsed and impenitent

     obstinate contumacious

she had no further hope

in the life of this world

THE DOVE

IT WAS SEPTEMBER—the first day—
and school was all worked up with Joan's return. That
morning everyone enacted caricatures of themselves,
laughing louder, speaking more, fading further
into the furniture of the hallways. I did the same, I
couldn't help it, like this grand play was a contractual
element of enrollment. We, the assigned; Joan, our
witness. Holding books to my chest, I performed my
studiousness and seriousness, my piety. I smiled at the
kids I knew and waved cautiously to my friends from
last year. They waved back and maybe their faces were
contorted, maybe they laughed when I turned but that
was ok, because Joan was here, was somewhere in this
brick two-story building. The five-minute bell rang and
I went to the bathroom, trying not to look in the wide
mirror above the sinks because vanity was, as Father Joe
said, the most prevalent among sins. I was tempted and
looked quickly and pulled the hair-tie from the base of
my ponytail. I left the bathroom with my hair down but
I didn't see Joan anywhere.

I had watched Joan's videos each one hundred times.
Every morning when I woke, it was as if I'd dreamt
of Joan, their message, the flood; before my eyes even
opened, Joan was on the tip of my tongue, Joan's figure
on my phone screen, their silhouette imprinted onto

my narrow hand and in my headphones their voice was deep, resounding in my ears: the sun doesn't know about the night; the sun's never felt a shadow. I looked out onto the world and Joan's face lay right behind it, a shallow palimpsest of the truth.

And now Joan was back in school, back after a year away that only rumors could account for and now was in my class: an answer to prayers which I hadn't even known how to pray. God didn't speak to me but I knew this was a message: find and be close to Joan. Protect them. That morning, I bowed my head in thanks.

After homeroom, we all attended mass. The whole school sat in the pews, and though my old friends gestured, I gave a shrug and sat in the back. I scanned heads, looking for the short dark hair, the shape of the shoulders. My heart was loud as the church filled up, anticipation pulsed in my limbs, and another wave of students filed in. Then a shape in my periphery made me turn and I was staring: it was Joan, in the same row as me. Only a couple seats over. With an invisible signal, we all stood and I willed my eyes not to look, my body not to move. As the hymnals thudded open, my stomach plunged down to my pelvis.

"Blest are they, full of sorrow," the church began singing as Father Joe walked in with the altar boys. I joined, softly, daring myself to sing louder, to make Joan hear. If Joan heard my voice, I thought—I sang quietly but precisely, imagining my notes to be distinct among those many souls that filled the church.

I tried to hear Joan singing. I couldn't separate one song from another. And the lights were so bright. Never had the small stained glass windows looked so glorious, or the pale carpeted church so pure. Was this revelation? I couldn't feel my legs.

"Blest are they who suffer in faith," I sang and I thought I heard a loudening voice on my left. Father Joe stepped into the pulpit and raised both hands.

"In the name of the Father, and the Son, and the Holy Spirit," Father Joe said with his right hand rigid as a blade, forming the sign of the cross in front of him.

"Amen."

I knew God was here. I loved to think that They were watching me, listening, and I longed to hear Them back, as Joan did; all those vast thoughts, all day and night, thoughts so big and many my brain couldn't contain them, and I knew this—but what kind of bliss might that be. I didn't love my own small mind, my little inklings that sometimes layered, weaving and rotating. My mind was too small even for my own small thoughts: those that laced together, denying the linear, escaped me. I could sense them as I could sense my veins, those lines of conduit—but what they carried? Unknowable.

Do God and the devil know all the same things, I wondered, and then crossed myself to be sure no sin had manifested, no doorway through which the devil could glide, uninterrupted and all-knowing. Oh the devil certainly knew my sins, just as God did. The devil knew my lies and broken promises. My jealousies and vanities and the strange touching I did in the seventh grade with Sarah Hartnell behind the first line of pine trees at the edge of the playground—how Sarah had gripped me, her small fingernails piercing the smooth skin on the inside of my upper arm. How my mom had complained to the school that someone was clearly bullying her daughter and I had to stop seeing Sarah, but I returned to those meetings behind the pine trees in my mind most nights. This, too, I could barely think. Mass was over, and everyone was filing out of the pews. I looked to my left, then all around, but Joan had gone.

*

People in town thought the world went easy on me and maybe that's true. The parishioners said I'm lucky, or blessed—or even went in grace. My dad made money, my mom made brownies, and Father Joe, despite my seventh-grade confessionals, said I'm a beacon of faith. Last year I was voted "Most Christ-Like" of Domremy Catholic High's freshman class.

I hoped that I did have God's grace to thank for my ease in the world. Something about grace, even though one need not do anything to receive it, denoted heroism. It was heroism in the sense of being singled out and chosen—an idea that accounted for and made tolerable the ways in which I felt entirely alone. Like maybe the ease with which the world met me was the result of my struggle with the greatest difficulty on earth: transcending it.

Nothing, I knew, had been easy for Joan—nothing except talking to God. "God responds when greeted with silence," they said in one of their videos. I had attempted silence in every form I could fathom but even my attempts felt loud. First question I had to ask Joan: how to empty myself of my self.

Mom had made cookies for me to share with any friends I still might have on the first day of school, and I held the tupperware open, my hand dipping up and down as other hands entered and plucked and I scanned the board with lists of all the classes for the semester.

First period math, then Spanish, lunch, etc. etc., and finally seventh period English: my name and, just above it, Joan's.

This had to be how God talked to people.

After everyone else entered the English classroom, I filed in. Joan was in the second row of desks and I didn't really think about it, I just sat in the seat behind them. The figure in front of me looked too big for the desk, even though Joan couldn't be much larger than me; their shoulders were broad in a button-down, and every limb jabbed out in a pose that looked imminently mobile. Joan's dark hair had grown during the year since the campaign, but it was rough, uncut and unstyled. Students wore uniforms at Domremy Catholic, but

Joan wore the boys' clothes. I guess no one in the school had thought to insist otherwise. Everyone was busy freaking out at the mere fact of them.

When Joan turned back to pass along a stack of papers, my ribcage contracted. Our eyes briefly met. Without looking at what the paper said, I turned it over and wrote a note in the corner, then carefully ripped it off and folded it.

This was the game: to do something brave before my body could think better of it. When the teacher turned toward the board, I tapped Joan's right shoulder. They turned, and their eyes were so dark that it was hard to meet their gaze. I held out the note. Joan took it and turned forward.

I thought I might die but God was watching. Joan was hunched over, and seemed to be writing. They looked up at the teacher before passing back the note without turning. I took it quickly, the tips of my fingers meeting Joan's, and never has the support of a chair been so useful. I read:

Hi Adrienne,
We sat near each other in church.
You have a nice voice.
Meet me by the gate after 8th period?
Joan

*

After school, we walked. The light was thin and it was cloudy. I felt every crack on the sidewalk, saw the swaths of dead grass newly; the street was quiet other than brush rustling, houses and garages humming, the moving air on the interstate miles away. I lived in Domremy proper, where the houses stood in neat rows and I could walk to the supermarket but Joan lived higher up in the valley, toward the edge of the county, which I knew because everyone knew: during the campaign, we all had to give directions to the reporters who came to talk to Joan. Father Joe told people to stop telling the truth. He said, Let the poor kid have some peace, but no one really thought Joan wanted it.

We walked on and uphill and were silent. Our wordlessness began to grow edges, and the pit I usually felt inside deepened. Every moment was made of choices. Decisions that shaped the minutes of my life, and every hour the consequences of those moments multiplied. One morning I woke up, but the next morning I woke up and the AC was on. In the whole house, and in every house in town. My alarm was on my phone which contained cobalt from the Democratic Republic of the Congo and the air-conditioning was always on; the AC or the heat, and now that truth lived inside me every second. Sometimes I thought about it at school, too, but at school I usually thought about the dripping units in the classroom windows. And the lights, and the water, and the tanks of gas beneath the building. I thought about how gas trickled through the walls in mined copper pipes, walls of plasterboard and foam. Joan and I walked on asphalt made of oil and exploded earth that separated the dirt from rain, and it made floods heavier and summers hotter.

My dad and mom had big cars and the seats of Dad's were covered with the skin of cows from Brazil, where people were killing the rainforest, many people who had no choice. And Mom left our wooden house in her car with rubber tires and went to the grocery store with the big asphalt parking lot to get things for dinner, foods that were shipped there over oiled roads, vegetables picked and planted by people fleeing bad Warmth and bad governments, governments that my own had ruined.

And all the food we would eat was wrapped in plastic, which would live longer than me. The wrappers and containers would get old together, not alone like me, dead in the ground—my plastic would shine on in piles on land and sea. It would choke animals after I died. It would kill the cowbirds that were killing the songbirds, cowbirds that came south from the grasslands and laid their eggs in nests that weren't theirs. And when the cowchicklets hatched, they were full of want, and they took from the songbird's own young, starving them. I was a cowbird. My town was built by cowbirds. We would die in barren trees in a dead forest on fire.

Arkansas was on fire. From this high in the valley, Domremy looked swallowed by the drying-up Arkansas and Petit Jean Rivers and the mountains that cupped it. Mountains that were wearing down faster with fewer trees to shield them. And beyond that, in the northwest, the horizon was dark with smoke from the wildfires. I tried to cover up the pit inside and Joan looked over.

"You seem like a nice person."

Grace filled me. "You too." I breathed harder as we climbed. "Thanks for responding to my note."

"Thanks for watching my videos," Joan said.

A few moments later they asked, "Do you think it's a sin to use the pronouns of the Lord?"

"Not if you don't capitalize them," I said.

Even in the Warmth there were good days. Joan laughed and the sky was orange and the air felt cool. I tried to look at what I held, what manifested in my body. This was something I had learned from the internet, videos that I watched late at night when I couldn't sleep. As I walked with Joan, I located excitement, despair, vulnerability. Solastalgia, I thought, rolling the syllables in my mouth. There was anger, too, a fury that lived in my ribcage and compressed my breath. I suspected that my body resisted that rage, transmuting it into anxiety each time I let my mind follow the tendrils of anger out to their instigators in the world. I would twist the thoughts to join with other, softer problems, like buying a coral-reef-safe sunscreen or researching how to compost or finding vegetarian recipes that even my parents might like. This turning of my attention was wrong, I knew—or too easy, as in, not quite truthful—

yet the anger and anxieties blended until my panic subsumed into semblant ease.

But Joan understood. We had barely shared seven sentences, but I knew that Joan understood and that I understood them too.

"Nearly there," Joan said.

Suddenly I felt violent, heady, as if the endless uncertainty that had blurred me was suddenly chiseled to a point and aimed at Joan. I wanted them to know every part of me, to compress the space between us, to confess every thought and sensation so that the truth would tether us together. If only I could tell Joan everything—and by telling them everything I would tell only the truth.

We turned onto the driveway of a single-story brick house. There wasn't a car parked out front and Joan paused only to drop their backpack on the back porch, directing me to do the same. They led us through the backyard and into the forest.

The trees were different here, I thought. Under the dense green canopy, Joan pointed to different trunks. "Red oak, white oak, hickory. That's a maple-leaf oak, which only really grows in the Ouachitas," they said.

I didn't know the last time I'd been in the woods. Microbes in the soil increase the release of serotonin in the brain, I knew from the internet, but never had

I acted upon that information. We followed a narrow path that was scarcely discernible from layers of fallen branches and leaves and undergrowth. I breathed in. "It smells so good here."

"It's an old-growth forest," Joan said, turning back to look at me. "There's centuries of humus beneath us."

"How do you know so much about this?" I asked.

"My mom's a park ranger. And the voices told me about it."

In the heavy shadows of the forest, Joan started to cry. Overwhelm crashed through, and small sounds surrounded them, joining Joan as their cries turned to sobs; the wind, small mammals in undergrowth and on branches, birds leaving the canopy for open sky. I located some small part of myself that felt relief: my purpose here was clear. I touched Joan's arm gently, and when they didn't move away, I stepped toward them. I wrapped my arms around their thin frame. We were the same height, and I dropped my chin to rest on Joan's shoulder.

Slowly their chest stopped heaving, slowly they relaxed their body into mine. They put their hands around my waist before looking at me with their wet face.

"I'm sorry."

"You don't have anything to be sorry for."

Joan smiled ruefully. "But I do."

*

"Are you sure it's ok?" I asked. They had asked if I wanted to stay for dinner.

Joan laughed. "You kidding? My mom is going to be thrilled."

"Mine too," I said. As long as my mom didn't know who my new friend was. I texted my parents for permission and my mom quickly assented, texting, *Of course, that's great honey. Do you want me to pick you up after?*

"Do you think your mom could drive me home after dinner?" I asked Joan.

"Sure, I bet that's fine."

I wrote, *No, thanks though. They'll give me a ride back.*

Joan's mom was shorter than Joan, and a bit rounder, which wasn't hard. Mostly she had a really kind face.

"Adrienne, so nice to meet you! Call me Izzy," she said.

"Thank you so much for having me."

"Of course, honey. It's good to have a new face around here. Is spaghetti ok?"

Izzy didn't change out of her ranger's uniform, but started boiling water and rummaging through the cabinets while Joan and I went out to the garden in the side yard. I hadn't noticed it before: six raised boxes, the dirt dark between the vegetables.

"Nearly the end of lettuce season, but there's still some good leaves," Joan said.

"This is so cool."

"Thanks. My mom obviously did all the planting this year since I was gone. And she never gets the spacing right!" Joan finished loudly.

"I can hear you!" Izzy shouted through the open window above the kitchen sink.

I couldn't remember an evening of such calm, of such surreality. This was happiness, I thought, and time receded even as I longed for every evening to be this evening; I wanted not a repetition of this day but its literal return. Twilight turned to night and the garden was lit from the warm glow of the kitchen window.

Maybe this was faith: the substance of things you didn't even know to hope for—the void filled with certainty in the absence of doubt because doubt, like darkness, has no substance. The dark night outside was just the absence of light. My phone vibrated. I didn't look.

When we reentered the house, the local news was on in

the living room. The TV suddenly flashed an image of President Charles, then a video from a press conference. "Well, my administration is in support of good jobs in every sector, including clean coal and the sustainable harvesting of our natural resources," he said. Izzy quickly emerged in sweat pants and turned off the TV.

"I'm so sorry, baby. I was trying to listen to the news on this year's hunting season," she said to Joan, who was staring at the blank screen with the bowl of vegetables in their hands. They shook themselves.

"It's ok."

"But it's not," she said.

Joan was quiet during dinner, and their mom gently filled the space by asking me questions. I could tell they were meant to be easy, just comfortable small talk, but nothing felt straight-forward. My classes, clubs, and college plans felt irrelevant. The old growth trees on fire filled my mind. The sound of Joan crying, the way their hands felt holding my waist.

After dinner, Izzy drove me home. Joan had given me a hug then went to go do the dishes, their head bent low over the sink as their shoulders shook.

"It was so nice of you to come over," Izzy said after she started the car. "It's been a hard couple of years for them."

"I wanted to," I said, trying to identify the reason for my discomfort. Didn't she know how Joan had changed my life?

"They have their good days, but sometimes—you know, it's still difficult," she said.

"Of course."

"You're a good kid, Adrienne."

I was quiet for moment. "You seem like a really good parent."

"Oh! Well, thank you," she said, seeming embarrassed.

I felt embarrassed too, but I meant it.

My mom greeted me from the sofa and I ran up the stairs. Streetlights glared into my bedroom window. I texted Joan: *What are you doing tomorrow after school?*

They had probably finished cleaning the kitchen. Soon Joan's mom would walk through the door, ask them about their first day back. I spread my homework on the bed and changed. My phone was dark and quiet. I filled out the worksheets and read a chapter for English and laid out tomorrow's uniform. I brushed my teeth, and my mom came in to say goodnight. She turned off the lights before she closed the door. I kneeled by the edge of the bed to pray.

My eyes closed and my phone lit up.

Can I do whatever you're doing?

*

Never had a season passed so quickly. With Joan, I attended to each change in the temperature, foliage, and wildlife. My attention seemed to speed time rather than still it; each leafed-tree turned golden and red and Joan walked beside me. The sky was orange but not black and every day we went to the forest and the geese flew south and the world filled up the void inside me.

I kissed Joan now against red oaks, white oaks, hickories. We lay beneath maple-leaf oaks, my knee between their thighs and their mouth finding the skin of my sternum. On days that it rained, Joan and I would run in our raincoats to Joan's empty house and do homework, tend the garden while holding umbrellas for each other, cook dinner to surprise Izzy when she got home from work. The days became colder, and we took a blanket from Joan's house to huddle in the fallen leaves.

*

I woke one morning with a sore throat. Smoke from the mountains had flooded down into the valley. The other side of the river was shrouded and Domremy felt shrunken, diminished by its sudden lack of context. School was canceled and I stayed in bed.

This feels like the end of the world, I texted Joan.

Except everyone will go back to school in a couple days and act like nothing happened.

As if the world wasn't literally on fire.

*

"I need to tell you something," Joan said.

At the edge of the trees, a cottontail bounded toward us then froze. I knew the feeling: only the right gaze felt good; only with love did it feel safe to be singled-out.

"I'm leaving," Joan said. They were joining the Forest Service, a wildfire crew, they were headed to the northwest state border. Izzy would drive them. She had helped Joan get the job, even though she hated it. But Joan was old enough, they could leave school, wear a new uniform.

Joan was leaving and they were just telling me now. They hadn't told me until just now and what was I supposed to do. I couldn't go with them. We'd be alone in the woods with new canopies of smoke.

The sun was bright despite its weak winter angle. My face and hands and feet were cold. The burning trees would be dead for the rest of my life and Joan was leaving. I wouldn't even pass them in the hallway. Something tore from my chest.

No voices had ever guided me, I had always been forsaken. Or this was a sign from God. Joan was gone. I couldn't breathe. Gravity overwhelmed me, swallowing until its presence was totalizing, then negating. I realized my eyes were open and I was on my knees, branches digging into my skin and my tights were ripped. My hands were covered in dirt. I couldn't feel my limbs and Joan was crying on their hands and knees in front of me, pleading with me to understand. They loved me, they promised. They loved me so much. They would come back, they needed me, but they had to try to save something. They couldn't save us but maybe they could save something.

They couldn't save anything. Joan stood in firefighting gear at the edge of the forest, dried-up blackberry brambles caught on their coat. It was the other side of Ozarks: pine and chicory, fast-burning. The orange sky was no longer sky but a dark fiery plume as tall as it was wide. The forest floor was fire, each tree a lit match toward heaven.

I knew they would burn. I knew how it began, briefly, in pleasure: that warmth like the mother, the lover, the home, the hearth; Joan had known it all, they had known me and left, their warm hands holding my face, their lips on mine and their cheeks wet and pressed against me but there was fire.

Do not fear what you are about to suffer. Fire from the altar thrown down to earth.

The pleasure was quick, crystalline, soon searing. I knew about fire, how it gave way to pain so sharp I felt limbless, the stench savory—it was my own feet that burned, the skin recoiling, leg hairs catching like pine needles, bright sparks as the Heat reached into muscle. The water in my body steamed; I was a crater, a pitted void left after tectonic action; still smoking as the rest of my cells gave way—cilia, cell wall, nucleus. Mere feeling. My eyes were still open, and I looked up. I saw a white bird fly out of the trees.

I love you so much, They said.

ACKNOWLEDGEMENTS

In his book *Warmth: Coming of Age at the End of Our World*, Daniel Sherrell demonstrates that the existing words serve only to flatten "the Problem," as he calls it; no words are good enough, and especially not the ones we use now. Sherrell's book helped me to let go of existing language and thereby feel the grief that I had previously compartmentalized into distant concept.

Here is a list of other books that deeply informed this project: Jean Anouilh, *The Lark*; Anne Carson, *Autobiography of Red*, *Bakkhai*, and *Norma Jean Baker of Troy*; Theresa Hak Kyung Cha, *Dictee*; Don Mee Choi, *DMZ Colony*; Inger Christensen, *Alphabet*; Cody-Rose Clevidence, *Aux/Arc Trypt Ich*; Amitav Ghosh, *The Great Derangement: Climate Change and the Unthinkable*; Françoise Meltzer, *For Fear of the Fire: Joan of Arc and the Limits of Subjectivity*; Lydia Millet, *A Children's Bible*; Elaine Scarry, *On Beauty and Being Just*; and Mónica de la Torre, *The Happy End / All Welcome*.

The editorial collective at Ugly Duckling Presse gave me a reason to finish this project. Rebekah Smith's early edits were critical, and I am so grateful for the support of Michael Newton and Yelena Gluzman. Thanks to the working collective for everything.

The Whiting Foundation and the awards they give are incredible. To the anonymous nominator, judges, and to the entire staff of the foundation: thank you.

Without the enthusiasm and feedback of David Richardson and Ian Anderson, I might have delayed this book's publication another half year. Thank you to Dan Poppick, Claire Donato, and Cole Swensen. Thank you, Mónica de la Torre.

Emma Horwitz's play *Mary Gets Hers* was an inspiration in form and language and risky pleasures; writing is twice as satisfying knowing that she is in the world writing too.

By way of their own research and enthusiasm, Louise Akers compelled me to begin reading about Joan of Arc and to write unapologetically about angels. They and their book *Elizabeth/ Story of Drone* are brilliant.

Through her own grace in fiction and life, Madison Newbound eased me into vulnerable narratives and talked me through the hardest parts of this manuscript. Thank you for your genius, love, and for telling me to quit that job. I feel so lucky to share a writing life with you.

Finally, thanks to everyone who listened to me ramble about medieval understandings of reality and supported me nonetheless, and thank you to my parents and family. I couldn't have finished this book without my mom's friendship and support.